Goose Music

ANDY BROWN is Director of the Centre for Creative Writing at the University of Exeter. His recent books include *Fall of the Rebel Angels: Poems 1996–2006* (Salt) and *The Storm Berm* (Tall-Lighthouse). He studied Ecology, a discipline that informs both his poetry and his criticism, which appears in *The Salt Companion to the Works of Lee Harwood* (Salt). He edited *The Allotment: new lyric poets*, and *Binary Myths: Volumes 1&2* (both Stride). He was previously a Centre Director for the Arvon Foundation, has been a recording musician, and writes and has published numerous short stories.

JOHN BURNSIDE was born in 1955 in Dunfermline, Scotland. He studied English and European Languages at Cambridge College of Arts and Technology. A former computer software engineer, he has been a freelance writer since 1996. His first collection of poetry, *The Hoop*, was published in 1988 and won a Scottish Arts Council Book Award. Other poetry collections include *Common Knowledge* (1991), *Feast Days* (1992), winner of the Geoffrey Faber Memorial Prize, and *The Asylum Dance* (2000), winner of the Whitbread Poetry Award and shortlisted for both the Forward Poetry Prize (Best Poetry Collection of the Year) and the T.S. Eliot Prize. *The Light Trap* (2001) was also shortlisted for the T.S. Eliot Prize.

Goose Music

ANDY BROWN & JOHN BURNSIDE

CAMBRIDGE

PUBLISHED BY SALT PUBLISHING
14a High Street, Fulbourn, Cambridge CB21 5DH United Kingdom

© Andy Brown and John Burnside, 2008

First published 2008

Printed and bound in the United Kingdom by Biddles Ltd, King's Lynn, Norfolk

Typeset in Swift 9.5 / 13

ISBN 978 1 84471 284 7 hardback

Salt Publishing Ltd gratefully acknowledges
the financial assistance of Arts Council England

1 3 5 7 9 8 6 4 2

'In dire necessity somebody might write another Iliad, or paint an "Angelus", but fashion a goose? . . . If, then, we can live without goose music, we may as well do away with stars, or sunsets, or Iliads. But the point is that we would be fools to do away with any of them.'

— ALDO LEOPOLD

Contents

Acknowledgements

Acknowledgements are due to the editors of the following publications where some of these poems, or versions of them, first appeared: *Acumen; Bonfire: an international conflagration; Earth has not any thing to shew more fair* (Shakespeare's Globe & the Wordsworth Trust, 2002); *Echolocation* (University of Toronto); *Fire; Island Magazine; London Review of Books; Manhattan Review; NthPosition; Paris Review; Poetry Review; Popularity Contest; Proof; Sounding Heaven and Earth: a book of uncommon prayer* (Spire Trust, 2004); *Stride Magazine; The Argotist; The Red Wheelbarrow; A Journal of Prose Poetics, The Tall Lighthouse Review* 2006; *The Third Way; The Trust Territory* (Heaventree, 2005); *VOICE* (Dartington Ways With Words Festival, 2005) and *The Worple Catalogue.*

Part One

Goose Music

All morning the female greylag goose
stands in the chapel of her own stillness,
at the edge of the lido,
                            in a curd of mud,
while mergansers, herons, otters, mink,
come and go.
                    These are the lives.

Her mate budges,
                        wades into the pool,
its undulating surface washing up
wads of weed to the mud chute.

He eyes the distant vortex of the
watersluice and weir,
                            his feet dredging
globules of alluvial goo,
                                detritus,
seed husks and burrs
                        from the shallows,
where loaches feed;
                        where frogs and newts
will yield up their jelly
between tufts of *Juncus*.

A shade of gnats vibrates above
an umber hummock of dried sedge,
each a mere mote.
                    At your feet
a vetch uncurls;
the whelp of a vixen on the emery wind.

You have spent a lifetime
                        reading animals—

the scratchings of voles,
the golden spin of minnows,
a group of roe deer silent through the woods

but, as you pull your cagoule
over head—
                    in the moment
of that dark hiatus—
                                        she is gone,
the two geese up and running
over fresh water,
                                    ready for the sea—

miles to fly to feeding grounds
and hundreds more
to breeding grounds
                                    that spawned them,
across the great air masses,
this punishing travel,
to return and renew.

Some Notes on a Theory of Emergence

I

It starts before we see it:

coming inside from the garden, some February night,
wet snow fledging the walls and the idle

question that recurs, from time to time,
the one about birds, or frogs, or a year's worth of bees

cradled, somewhere,
in the crook of a shed, or a gable;

warm enough to harbour a beginning,
and softer than the voices that will come,

far in the wires
of this, or another, season,

still imperceptible, but all there is for now
of ripeness

and as urgent in itself

as any fruit: the glister of the seed
informing what it cancels, in a fall

that nothing can describe
until it happens.

II

Empty for miles, until
it found me, out on the plain,

and spilled its hidden freight
of light and quiver;

though how can we know that the wind
is silent till it comes across a shape

to keen against
—some animal, perhaps,

the musk ox stopped in its tracks
at the edge of a snowfall,

or something almost human in a drift
of moss and stone:
                    an echo in the land

becoming colour, texture, resonance;
the accident that gives itself a voice.

III

Forget the map;
forget the boundaries;

stand in the light
where willowseed blows through the wire

and listen:
            a pintailed duck
is calling, somewhere,
out along the fence

and somewhere else
the wind has taken shape:

a spill of poppies
sun-gold in the mist

and further
            on a hill-road white with stars

a man
becomes a flock of ptarmigan;

and every ptarmigan
becomes a man

IV

and here is the pattern, obeying a law
we forget:

            a winter's day in 1969;
frost on the pantry window; a father's voice

heading away from the house
where his children are sleeping

and
        suddenly
                    a shadow in the self
foresees this moment: windfalls in the grass,

and someone else come out,
to taste the dark;

and this is what we still mistake
for time

—the river run; the phases of the moon;
a spill of petals folding into stone

that emptiness between the sound of rain
and something in the roof that shift and slides,

alive, for now,
                    though neither bird nor beast,
but sea-shaped, salted, heavy as the tide.

v

Let me begin again in the powdered loam
I brushed aside to gather in a haul

of ants' eggs: nine years old,
a keeper of fish and secrets, I almost guessed

that everything was ordered by its own
momentum, as I rinsed away the sting

of formic acid, haunted by the maze
of angry bodies, patterns not quite seen

but felt, the way I felt the tug of things
at rest, or far at sea, lodestone and herring

tuned to the sway in the bone
that kept me whole.
                    Let me begin again,

just as I did that summer afternoon,
rain in the dust and the old pattern leaching away

pure revelation, like loss,
or the turn of the tide,

the hum in the bones of my wrist
and the itch in my fingers

promises still to be kept,
in an infinite world.

Nature Corner

I

Something from the classroom's edge
encroaches on us, as if on angels' wings,
fattening itself in our imaginations—
the promise of a metamorphosis
we long to share. The Cabbage-Whites
lay the neat tesserae of their eggs
beneath a scaffold of twigs and leaves.
Daily we observe and measure, sketch, record;
estimate how many eggs will hatch;
how many of the grubs may toughen up
impossible skins to leather cocoons,
glutted on greenery; their pupal pods
suspended by silk threads, each holding back
the secrets of a graceful transformation.

II

As martins slip out of a lazuli sky
alive with the play of migration, we thread
our way across the mud towards the byre,
your steps braiding with mine. The birds
return above a patchwork map of hills,
of rivers, deserts, coasts and plains,
to build mud nests beneath the eaves
and feed their growing brood, their wisps of need.

The martins scintillate the air to heat ripples.
Aerial artistes, they weave the cords that link
a gnu's back and a cow's. How can we wrest
their secrets from them; know where they are
in their bodies? Together, we watch them nest,
their arcs of flight vibrating in our fingers.

III

Bugling in flight, the greylags leave in V's—
two grey scarves trailing in the wind.
They run across the water; lift into the breeze—
'You have wings on your back. Wings!'

The geese hang by threads of their own making,
over scalloped fans of lakes until
they come to land in an *elsewhere*, bowing
to gravity, inexorably, like apples.

IV AS THE TIDE SUCKS OUT AT DAYBREAK

the plash and waft of washed-up kelp
reveals black rocks that fling slant edges high.

From our rug beside a radiant gorse
we hear the grating cackles of the shag roost;

great fulmars and tussock birds squabbling
on ledges, while pipits unwind their songs.

Through spray-haze the combers arrive,
over the rotten timbers of the vessel—

her engines failed, her punctured hull sunk—
in search of the treasures that hang like grapes,

bunched in blue on her sand-banked flanks:
the thrill of finding; the mystery of prizing open;

everybody focused, underneath the spell,
locked into the morning hunt for mussels.

V IN CONVERSATION

This is the season of rut. Low pitched whines
rise to high crescendos, falling grunts.
Along a wooded stream, a Sitka black-tailed deer
noses the white skin at his mate's behind.

From aardvark to zebra the tongues of the kingdom
are waggling. We have made friends with the trout
spawning in the late Spring melt of water
that swells the brawling streams.

On a slate ledge higher on the hillside,
a goat choir sings the praises of the mountains:
'A garden is good as a prayer.' Sometimes, isn't it
just like everything wants to stop and talk?

Atavism

When chestnuts bloom and gardens
are fragrant
          with lilacs,
your mind,
             filled with pictures
taken by your eyes,
                cannot forget
the frescoes of chance;
the incomplete mosaics of forever
that bring us here;
                the actions of earth
that move great rocks;
ancient fauna
            traversing land bridges,
their bones and spoor
              hardening
in reed beds
          and layers of silt.

You can almost hear the grass
growing;
          touching something
in the snake of the spine —
this atavistic urge to find a home;
a pattern in the accidents.
                 Our prints
are not the only ones ever
to mark the riverbed and saltmarsh;
to find themselves
        preserved
          by falling ash;
to be set in concrete
            on the boulevard.

Sometimes, evenings, I sit up
and watch the dusk settle on
scrub slopes,
        copses,
                tuffs;

watch it settle on
                chains of streets
stretching far into the slanting light;
the greener ridges to the east—
a glow spreading over—

throwing things
                in sharp relief:
those footprints striding to the woods
and disappearing;
                the animal tracks
in cemeteries,
        rail embankments,
                fields and yards.

Insomnia

As a child, I would pray
to the patron saint of milk-floats

and the blackbird
that lived in the hedge

between my window
and the pit-head dawn.

Not that I asked for much
—it was mostly a case

of putting myself at ease
with the thought of receiving;

and, later,
when the world about me woke,

what I felt was the missing tree
at the end of the close,

the animals not in the woods,
the absence of linnets,

how everything I wanted was a dream
I'd borrowed from my mother's almanac,

the words for things
persisting, while they seeped

away, the new estates
and public schemes

assuming the names of the world
and making them old:

Willowbrook; Sycamore; Holly Tree;
Primrose; Fox.

The Other Garden

'The Puritans believed that, after the Flood, Eden still existed, scattered around the globe. They began to piece it back together, re-asserting Adam's 'mastery' of nature, by ascribing it names: Malus. Ficus. Homo sapiens.'

... but at the edge of all this neatness lies
the *other* garden—the dark world underfoot—
fallen fronds, wet bark and woody stems
returned to songs of rot beyond the border.

Look through the brittle skeletons of leaves;
inhale the humus' bitter-sweetness;
touch the velvet minarets of mushrooms.

Listen to the music of growth and decay—
we are not the only composers. The blackbird,
rooting out his meals above the compost,
raises songs without a thought of order;

no thought of naming anything at all;
yet every bit a part, as you and I,
of all that makes this garden, green, untamed.

Ganders in the Gardens

'The act of writing is for remembering what happens there at the
beginning, when we were children, seeing things and naming things in
wonderfully oblique ways.'
— KIM STAFFORD

These monolithic beeches are amazing
aren't they, the way their trunks support
the heavens in a memory of seed?

As they bud into full blade and beechmast,
their stained-glass shade is all too tempting:
children ignore the gardener's signs,

scoot over lawns with whoops and turn
quick circles round the silver giants—
their voices scaling branches, and then off,
to splash about in ponds and sculpted fountains.

They scatter a gaggle of geese from jade water
crying 'Gooses!'   There they go, our childhoods,
speaking to us of small things.   Honking,
clumsy ganders.   You just want to cuddle them.

A Horse's Skull

What we most loved in bone
was whiter there,
washed by a season of rain, the hollows
darker than the black that fills the eyes
of fallen birds.

We left it to November afternoons,
left it to stand through Christmas, like the pearled
aftermath of gathered mistletoe,
lost it for weeks in the thaw, our wintered minds
attuned to crocus spears and scabs of moss,

only to find it later, stitched with grass
and spotted with the blue of moonless kills,
further along the fenceline than we remembered,
a damp hypothesis of earth and gas,
cradling the lace of stinkhorn or fly agaric.

On Hollow Moor

My eyes followed
                  your silence
across the early summer
morning,
          fine particles
                    of pollen in clouds
above the culm;
              its lush bunchgrass
now sun-dried
            and flagging
over the network of rivulets
in the deep down marsh.

The day was sear
and we had lain awake
all night,
        frightened,
                  like when we were children.

On a bluff at a bend in a stream,
pain splashed in
                of a June day,
riding across this
Hollow Moor
          to where you were.

I watched your knees go;
felt my knees
            give as well.

A heavy gate rocked
                    off its hinges . . .
the shimmering poplars
      the trembling aspens . . .

and somewhere an animal called,
    splashed,
                was gone
in eddies of grass.

Perhaps because the grass
was full of crickets—
        their strange shrieking—

or maybe just because
        this is a land
                that reveals itself
slowly,
        it dawned on us,
                    slowly,

like the smell of changing seasons,
or the presence of an unexpected
shadow
        or deer fawn
                    at your feet

that you were going down
with oceanlike swells,
as I flapped
            and flushed a pheasant
from the withered grass,

my toes sinking
                into the sponge of the bog

before we went home to ask 'why?'

the bones of a lost ewe
bleaching in the windrows.

Eleven Gift Songs

'Labor to feel the life of God in your soul; labor to make the way of God your own, let it be your inheritance, your treasure, your occupation, your daily calling. Labor to God for your own soul as though there was no other creature on earth. Sweep clean. Ah, sweep clean I say. But, I say, sweep clean.'

—Testimonies of the Life, Character, Revelations and Doctrines
of Mother Ann Lee, and the Elders with Her

I EVENT

Nothing, or everything, matters;
new snow; the light on the asphalt

orange or cherry-red
when the quiet is over;

the car at the end of the street
completing its turn;

a girl walking home from school;
a man with his dog;

how pure occasion
sanctifies the world:

one thing and then the next,
then nothing at all

other than making space
for the life that continues,

the child you have still to name,
the tree in your garden,

this florist's window
lit before the dark:

its perfect golds
its subtleties of rose.

II COLOUR

In my mind's eye, the snow is falling on shingled walls;
a woman is washing a corpse in a lamplit kitchen;
someone has stopped at a gate, to offer the dog
a sweetmeat;
                    and, far in the distance,
the blue of a pine is the sum of the visible world;
enough, when it disappears, to begin again:
yellow, then silver; lilac, then tangerine.

III TIME

We had started to feel at home
in these names and skins:

Thursday: the girl from the crescent
walking to school in the dark

with her blinded viola;
Saturday afternoon like a halted bell

and that feeling we had
that nothing would ever happen,

waiting for hours at a time
in the hush of our lives

and watching the weather come in
as if we had planned it:

light in the trees
at the opposite end of the park;

water and falling snow
and a Nazarene sun.

IV SPEECH

What do the dying remember,
if not the unspoken?
The intimate fog of scripture, the nightjar's call,
a hint of the yellow to come
in a bowl of persimmons?

As children we had words for how the sun
investigates the surface of a glass,
words for the mesh of a net, or how a shoal
of fishes in their millions, far at sea,
glamoured the sky;

now everything is absent from its name,
florist's shop, asphalt, snow pouring off a tree
and splashing across a pavement, like melting lace:
event, not noun; the transitory
event of the world slipping by, and the world is all.

V ASHES

Though they say it is only
the white of the brain burning out

and not the first tentative steps
to afterlife,

I want to be sure, when it comes,
that I see the light

exactly for what it is: no more or less
illusory than any other light

and surely no more illusion than the dark
where souls go floating, burning out like smuts,

or glimmering a moment in the heat
between a rice field and the coming stars.

VI GRAVITY

Imagine the world recovered in a touch:
every cobweb of a patient childhood;
fig trees in empty courtyards; mingled cries
and powdered wings along the arteries.
Imagine it: the forms that rise through ash,
the slow curve of a memorised caress
finding the bone and tracing out the lines
of marrow, for that angle in the flesh
where dust remains to name itself again.

VII REBIRTH

It's Kipling who says it, I think,
perhaps in *The Light That Failed*, where
the hero (whose name I forget)
stares at himself in the mirror and says out loud

'Never go back'.
            Though maybe it's someone else,
in another book,
coming to quiet grief, or the faint resignation
of one who has seen enough

to accept defeat.
            Though it's only defeat
while we're calling it something else,
and going back is only the mistake
we count upon, the key that turns the lock

on some far household in the mind itself:
your long-lost raincoat hanging in the hall
and the garden you know from a dream, in an empty mirror,
the holly bush filling with light and the flicker of swallows.

VIII ANACHORESIS

You have the right to remain silent;

also the right to choose
the company you keep;

if only the dead, then the dead:

poems and bookplates;
love songs whispered through static.

IX THE LIFE OF OTHERS

This morning, near the harbourfront, I passed
the undertaker walking to his car,
dressed for the job, but smiling, without that far
off look in his eyes, to show he'd seen the last

of human goodness decked out for the grave
in Sunday best: good wives and honest men,
the likes of whom will never come again.
Or is it just a cigarette he craves

when, standing by the hearse, he tries to seem
not unconcerned, but absent at the scene
of someone else's grief? He looked so glad

to be so by himself this morning, as the sun
singled him out: alive, in his own dream,
and no one there to counter but the dead.

X GARDEN

Summer is ending here, in a drift of smoke:
damp on the walls of the vine-house; mildew and cracks

in the paintwork, where a spider's nest has long since
broken;
       wisps

of gossamer and chitin left behind
like clues to something wider: life itself,

a thousand starlings settled on the roof
and walls, a hapless spill

of pinion-bones and feathers; butcher's broom
and eucalyptus, waiting for the fog.

Out on the meadows, someone is tending a fire;
no one I know, though a shape in his back

is familiar: the care he takes,
the way he holds his rake

familiar, like a sheath-knife or a scythe,
the way it fits the hand, the easy

heft of it.
He does his work the way it should be done,

the way that I would do it, with as little
movement as is needed, and the grace

that comes of being unaware of skill
or effort, and at ease within a world

where nothing else can happen for an hour
but this: the tended flame, the summer's end,

dew on the shaft of the rake
and the light on his hands

turning to gold, then green
as the evening surrounds him.

XI THE AFTERLIFE

Sooner or later, you wake in a different season,
the trees you can see from your window, the public gardens,
the bus stop where you disembarked last night
in summer clothes, with music in your head,
buried in snow today, and still, like the cities in snapshots.

How quickly it seems familiar, being dead:
that feeling of a public holiday
in winter; how the time it takes to cross
an empty street, all ridged and scarred with ice,
is suddenly too long; how far away

the others seem, sketched in as afterthoughts
—menfolk in hats and scarves, the hint of a girl—
smudges of water and ash on the morning light,
arriving from nowhere, mistaking themselves for a world.

Small Voices

If butterflies are the souls
of lost children, and meadow grasses
growing strong through dry stone walls—
Timothy,
      Brome,
           Sweet Vernal—
the ladders by which they ascend,

then we must be accompanied
by so many vanished, this June,
at the edge of the spinney,
butterflies all about us,
as we part veils of grass,
our hands pushing through
like swimmers' palms
               turned outwards,
beneath birches, budding oaks,
to find there,
      buried deep:
           mushrooms—

the *boletus* we gather with a twist
of their small white skulls;
           the *chanterelles*
a tug at their soft orange ears,
brushing off weevils and mites,
to return them
         to their tasks of decay.

When we are done, we check
fat berries forming on the briars,
ripening up for us,
       for birds this autumn.

From their nests in the dense copse,
the fledglings already have flown
and above—a form of clarity
themselves—swifts dancing.

Between us and our two children,
the day's last butterfly
                         disappears;
giving way to evening's
                         moths,

their flutterings outlined
by the unheard vibrato
                         of hunting bats;
our sundown yard
                 filled with froglets—
this place they all must leave
and some return to
next year
         and the next year still,
the vim of their small voices
moving from puddle to pond.

Pine Trees at Five Ways

The morning emerges in a counterpoint
of sun and mist;
                    a day streaming into
their branches.
                    They stand rooted
into the vertical,
like a Giacometti string quartet
talking things over musically
in a deep shaft filled with light.

On my hand your fingers;
on your face my eyes,
our tongues silent
in the vacuum
                    of a Sunday walk;

the spaces our bodies inhabit
defining spare geometries,
like the ring of the bells
in empty towers
                    from here to Iken Marsh.

On the brow of a rise,
the pilots of two stunt kites
hang their souls on hooks of air.

From the edge of the mere,
the morning calls of unseen creatures
like oboe players lost in the reeds.

For a moment it's no longer clear
who is walking towards whom;
                    us, or the trees?

Los ángeles mohosos

Cuerpo que por alma,
El vacío, nada.

— RAFAEL ALBERTI

I

They sing of an absolute night
and how we arrive from nothing: absence of fiat
and something like the wind, unpacking stars;

and, later, when they wake the animals,
the names are perfect, kindled from new skin
or falling from the darkness: plumes and sparks
of blindness; motion; pure inconstancy.

II

This is where cold begins,
and the cold light of Sabbathday mornings

run through the fence posts and pines
like the blue of a wire;

though later,
when I meet it in the yard,

shaped to the blade of a saw,
or the curve of a shovel,

it seems to come from nowhere, like the angel's
lifelong annunciation:

thawglass and stonework; wishbone
and flensing-knife;

whins in a remnant of wall, or a scatter of snail-shell
waiting for the wind to break it down.

Three Enquiries Concerning Angels

after Paul Klee

I GEIST DER SCHIFFER

The angels that come in the night
are thinnest
        and could be mistaken

for shadows,
        like the blackness in old coins
or scraps of dialect.

They slip through when no one is watching;
        sometimes they leave
handprints
        or a trail of talc and myrrh

but never enough
        to scare us
as these creatures of the day

who might even be what they seem
        —the greengrocer's son,
the woman who cleans for the doctor—

these terrible, sweet
        faces at the window,
seemingly

indifferent,
        against the yellow light

touched by a sudden warmth
        like pieces of litmus,

everyday people
     with somewhere else to go:
street sweepers, schoolboys,
the fishmonger's wife,

handling the things of the day
     but awake to the sky.

II WACHSAMER ENGEL

—one definition of grace
they hover against our doors, but never come

to rest;

not messengers at all,
  but

messages
  made flesh

—or, rather,
cartilage and feather
  blood and song,

fixed to a point or a moment
  no matter how far

they wander:
  windows and open
hallways;
  lamplight and flames

attract them
  though they never see themselves

as we do: chosen,
  ahistorical,

falling away from the surface,
 falling away

while light decays
 and form returns to dust.

III ENGEL, ÜBERVOLL

For years it was secret;
        then, one night,
it lights a lamp

and stands at an upstairs window,
looking out
at something within and beyond

its own reflection;
and what we mistake for the self
        has withered away,

replaced by a body
that asks
        what the world would ask,

something fine-tuned and immense,
        its flourish of light
a shape for the wind,

        a shape
for the orioles' singing.

I think of the people we are
        in the hour before dawn,

the long conversations we have
        when the rain is unending,

the silence we happen upon
        in the litmus of snow,

and nothing is really precise,
　　　　though a phrase heard in passing

can make it seem the world is possible
again : a world of memory and light

I carried so long
　　　　though I knew
there was nothing to carry.

The Ice Pool Under the Church Tower

signals a lingering winter,
                                    just as swallows and cuckoos
signal spring;
                        the steady accretions
of incognito flocks perched in the furze,
pocking dark fields,
their presence a subtle shift,
like summer falling into autumn;

or redwing and fieldfare
                                    from Norway and Siberia
escaping the harshness further north
on summer visits heading south
for Africa and the easy life
on the backs of wildebeest and zebra.

Starling flocks in their bubbles of air, startle
the dolmen henge of cattle
when they lunge into January flights
with a crack like the slap of burlap
                                    snagged on hawthorn,

but the ice rink under the church tower signals
winter persistent—
solitary dun migrants
                                    arcing the western wing;
shadowing hummocked graves,
the knobbed, flinted apse.

Prayer

The wide open places; benign
indifference to what we wish and fear.

Give us the shape in the mist that is always
moving, yet never appears
to approach or recede;

give us the cold wing
hovering over the waters;

the hush on the taiga;
the held breath filling the woods.

Verde que te quiero
                give us
what happens; what arrives; what goes unseen

and permit us this day
to love what we cannot love;

untouchables given in wedlock
to hay-bales and needles.

Prayer / Why I am Happy to be in the City this Spring

for creepers etched
    across a wall
    like the marble veins
    on *David*'s hands;

for the lichen, moss
    and granite blocks
    of the city's ancient
    battlements;

for empty paint pots,
    loose blue string
    and slightly sparkling
    bottled water
    discarded in the bushes,
    its dregs—quite still—
    reminding us
    we're only passing through;

for a builder's skip
    of silver crucifixes;

for sunlight on
    the golden rooster
    of a weathervane;

for a metal dragon
    listening
    to jingling cash
    outside the new café;

for students drinking coffee—
    their notes taking off
    in the wind;

for bird song
    when a door slams;

for birch trees
    like Elizabethan ladies
    painted white;

for the burgeoning stems
    of *Aloe Vera*
    in municipal gardens
    like chubby children
    playing *Stuck-in-the-mud*;

for water in a concrete pond;

for reflections,
    fish
    and ripples
    over grey;

for buttercups emerging
    through drain holes;

for garden planters
    standing bare all winter,
    now filled;

for distant hills;

for the balm of a snail's track
    on galvanised railings
    at midnight;

for this ongoing twilight
over our new home
and through it
the relief of seeing
individual stars.

Castor / Pollux

Then he was gone, and I followed his trail in the sand:
moths in the stitching of night and the scent
of oleander, threaded to the wind,
and somewhere beyond, the permanent loophole of water
—sandpipers massed in the reeds like one vast body;
avocet venturing out in the purl of the tide—

but nothing else: no echo in the world
that I could recover,
only the given stars in the given night,
a wide brocade of scorpions and dogs,
fishes and serpents, everything intertwined
as thought is,
                              though the space between the names
was void and cold.

I stopped, then, in the silvering of dawn,
something abandoned sewn to my lips and hands
like a phrase or a password I knew from another time,
a call from some childhood game, or a mother's warning,
wind on the meadow, the black sea turned on its axis,
the last faint stars receding in the blue
and I amongst them, cleaving to the sky.

Fiat Nox

Because I came to love the rule of snow,
the back door open on a winter's night

where someone had gone out to fetch the coal,
my mother's wireless talking to the dark

in Fifties language: everything
considered, guileless, unimpeachable;

because I would have looked up at the sky
to see the patterns other people saw,

kin with the dead and gone
and the not yet living,

I go out in the small hours with a pair
of old binoculars, to find the stars,

and walk away to where the streetlight ends,
dark at the edge of the sea and the land behind me

quiet, like a sleeping animal
and, overhead, no different from thought:

Cassiopeia; Pisces, Canes Venati;
The Bear, The Plough, The Serpent's Tail, The Swan.

Janus—Li Po Sonnets

The dunes across the estuary
recede to blue, like last year.
Windsurfers whip over wave peaks;
gusts slapping their sails to drums.

Children scuff foam near their parents,
turn and dash along the tide.
Above the spray, a cormorant
fights headwinds in false takeoffs.

II LITTORAL

The curving channel lies marked-out
with buoys. The turquoise bay crooks
beyond the drowsing dunes. We watch
boats haul in nets—lateen-sailed

booms hanging gracefully over
the waves—the simplest design.
Memory here could overflow
their bushel-baskets of clams.

III SCHOOLYARD

Through January rain, the church
delivers an old lesson
on the value of perspective,
gazing down from its steeple.

Stems and husks of *tangutica*
threaded through the old wire fence
reveal birds, calling the children
out to play, their faces raised.

IV PARK

The sun spills its indifference
across the city rooftops.
The bare peaks of copper beeches
revel in its viscous rays.

Footballs slap concrete walls, bounce free.
As conspiracies of teens
huddle on benches in smoke-clouds,
a lost ball bobbles downhill.

Orange

The heaven of childhood had something to do with citrus:
back in the coal towns, deep in a season of rain,
or out on the farm roads, away from the dangerous world,
where children came down from their attics, with sleep in
       their mouths,

light on the kitchen walls on a Christmas morning
and, under the tree, in their scarlet and matt-black wrappers,
the newborn clementines that flaked and scaled
like moths' or angels' wings between our fingers,

then melted to pulp and a liquor that darkened our palms
with the colour and scent of Jesus, raised from the dead
and walking alone in the garden, untouched by the future,

the light of the world returned, as he raises his hand
to gather a fruit from the darkness and taste, once again,
the blood-orange sap, the sweet at the heart of the bitter.

Part Two

Two Essays on the Folk Story

I THE LOST BOY

Someone—a sister perhaps—
has led him away from the house
in the morning fog:

older than him, and not
his sister at all, but
the child of his mother's husband, that

thin-lipped rake
she married in haste
when his father was lost at sea.

His pockets are full
of birdseed and broken glass;
his face is a mirror; his words and his silence

are mirrors;
and why he follows, when he half-suspects,
is most of what he is, the only one

in all of this
who proves himself
deserving.

Later, perhaps,
he turns around
and the one thing he always

expected, the one thing he probably
hoped for
has come to pass.

Not that he ever thought
about being alone
till now, with the shadows advancing,

playful and ready to strike, the animal
shadows, impossibly sweet,
like that sweetness he knows

from a dream, or from rising at dawn
and hearing the geese passing through
in a widening sky.

Of course, he has the thoughts
one might expect:
who knew? and: who agreed

to leaving him defenceless in the woods
where no one else will come, since this
is narrative, and snow is on the way

and something cruel he's known about for years
is waiting at the tree-line for the flaw
in everybody's logic—his, and mine

and yours—
reduced to memory and scent
and something in the flesh that welcomes death,

watching it come from the darkness
and into the clearing,
as small and no less precise than it looked in the field guides,

but lit
with its own green fire,
like the blood in a stone.

II THE SEVENTH SON

No matter how well they began,
the stories they told always led
to a colourless place,
a room without shadows or fire,
or a turn in the road
where everything I hoped for
disappeared,

and still no sign
of ocelot
or mink,
no stark face
catching my eye
when I bent to the water.

They say I walked for years,
asleep and waking,
drenched to the bone,
or burned
by the noonday sun,

but never met
the liar at the crossroads,
or whispered to the sphinx,
like one in love,
the answer to the riddle,
which was neither

true, nor false,
but somewhere in between,
like memory
or what I think of now
as perfect,
stealing back into the dark,
to rest a while
beneath my parents' roof,
where everything keeps watch,
but nothing sees.

The Breaking of Waves

I MERMAN

Beyond the Ness the fish-hands haul in nets.
Bald, with ragged beard and seal-skin naked,
some say the *thing* can shed his tail at will;
on land appears as all but human. The gillies
hand him over to the Governor, whose questions
he deflects in tongues of Cod and Plaice. In church
he shows no signs of Christian reverence.
They hang him by his feet and beat him senseless
with withies. He bears their torture silently,
eats nothing but Rollmop and Oyster,
month on month, preserving his wildness until,
lonely for his kind, he breaks away to sea,
flicking out the razor of his tail
to scythe across their fields of creels and nets.

You flip off the side
                        in a clear lagoon
between islets
                    on the oceanic shelf;
sink,
        kitted in the diver's dense caboodle,
flippers, wetsuit,
                        valves and nozzles,
down past anemone beds,
bright clots of jelly clinging to the rocks,
where whelks and winkles
                            graze meadows
of sea lettuce,
                coralina,
                            undulating weed—
down into open waters,
                        jacuzzi warm,
and into the turquoise cruising grounds
of nautilus, mako,
                    walrus, manatee;
through the dim megalopolis of kelp,
and beyond—
                the ocean
                            bottomless—
brother to the beluga,
                        snug in your blubber.

≈

... and then they hoist you up into cool air,
ready with the tank to save you from
       those   bubbles   in the   blood.

You blink,
           your pupils
                 readjusting;
stare at them through Cyclops mask
and wait for news
             from *this* world. . .

for every time they pull you up
they tell you something   major;
something   oceanic. . .

as though your trips down there
could conjure changes;
as though each surfacing might be
a second birth —

'He's coming now
            I see his head'

— your bubble-trails delivering you
from your origins at sea
into the ache of the air,
like a gaffed fish hauled on board,
as you hang on the line of their words,
your mind still fanning the seabed
with rays and flatfish,
                 pouting groupers,
conger eels reclusive in their haunts,
your thoughts ensnared
             in bladderwrack;

like the time you took your mask off
to be told
                'The Princess has died',
'the Twin Towers fallen',
'Kabul Flattened',
                        'Baghdad Changing Hands',
wondering what the news might be
this time,
                next time,
                        closer in to home . . .

III BALLAD OF THE UNDINES

(i)

'The war was (remotely) gearing up',
fishermen conscripted to the naval fleets
and the sea—that was the start and end
of all men knew; that measured time

by daily tides and herring runs
and missiles launched and warships sunk—
the sea gave sustenance to men but, in return,
she also sometimes claimed men back.

That sea was the *Persian Gulf*; the *Dead Sea*
and *Aegean*; the *Red Sea* and the *North*;
from where these fishermen returned from war,
the shelling of cities from battleships

and *theirs* the orders to fire the guns.
But when the sea was calm and men at home,
their families climbed the torch-lit path
to church, to thank the sea and sing its praises.

(ii)

One evening when the working boats relaxed,
the people at song and all the fish beneath,
something rose there in the harbour:
a girl, a fish, a daughter of the sea king *Llyr*

who'd heard some say that war was gearing up.
She broke the water's lens to rest on rocks,
tuning in to waves and wind and, on the wind,
the sound of the fisher folk singing.

She was the daughter of the Oceanid *Rân*,
the mother of maelsroms; the Queen of the Sea;
whose daughters—the Nine Waves of Oceans—
were born from foam and danced on water:

Ariel or *Atargatis*; *Dagon* and *Euromyne*;
Havfine; *Lenore* and *Melusina*;
Vodyany or *Vatea* the half-porpoise;
Sedna the Inuit and *Sirena* the Guam.

(iii)

The evidence for war, some said, was mounting;
but the next night and the next night still
Melusina wandered back, surfacing
by anchored boats to listen to the hymns.

'Whose voice is that to thrill such song?'
she asked, but there was only silence in return
and Melusina felt the waters pull,
knowing she must now return or strand.

Down she dove to the cave of Llyr,
to tell her father all that she had heard—
King Llyr, carved from flotsam;
his scales, his green tangles.

At Melusina's words he shook his head:
'That music is the music of a Man;
'and there you *must not* go. They sing and then
'wage war. And war, some say, is gearing up.'

Melusina cried: 'Then I shall wither away,
'for I would rather hear a Soldier sing
'than Whales!' And King Llyr sighed:
'Go! Go! But go with care. Cover your tail

'beneath a dress, such as their women wear.
'Take care that no one sees you.
'Return by high tide, or never return.'
Excited, Melusina: 'No one shall snare *me* like a cod!'

And she took the dress her father offered;
a dress he had transformed from skin of seal,
that covered up her tail and, so disguised,
she set out for the church and land of men.

(iv)

King Llyr then wept long at her leaving
while Melusina struggled to the church—
her tail, her dress—hauling herself from tree
to tree, arriving for the final hymn.

With their eyes in their hymnbooks,
none saw Melusina. But she saw them.
And one man seemed to her as though an angel.
And when he sang it was as though an angel.

She sighed, the whisper of the shore, enough
for him to hear. He stopped his singing,
silenced by the look of her, and love for her,
for these things, like the cruelties of Man

to fellow Man, are certain to happen.
But Melusina, frightened, felt her tail
wither and turned away. 'Hold on!' he called.
The congregation's hymnals fell from laps.

Tangled in her dress, the mermaid tripped.
Her angel caught her. 'Stay!' he sang.
'Don't leave!' But tears salt as seawater
wetted her cheeks: 'I cannot stay. I am as Mer.'

The man stared—the tail-tip beneath her dress.
It did not matter to him, for he had seen worse:
women without legs; children without arms
and *his* the order to fire the guns.

He picked her up, her arms about his neck.
'Then I will go with you for, after everything,
'I would only be as you.' His people spilled
from church: 'Hold back!' they cried,

his mother too. But he was won by Melusina
and ran toward the sea with her, and she,
quick and clever, tore pearls from her dress
and flung them on the path. The greedy fishermen.

(v)

Only that man's mother still ran after.
The tide on ebb. The waters dark.
The man plunged in above his knees.
His mother caught his shirt, but on he pushed,

The sea around his waist and shoulders now;
the waters closing over him and over Melusina;
his mother left with just a thread between
her fingers; a cord like an empty fishing line.

And she wept like Rân, for she knew her son's soul
was sinking through her doorway—the *Maelstrom*—
that whirlpool in these cold high latitudes
of the *English Channel*, where war was gearing up.

Note: 'The war was (remotely) gearing up', is borrowed from Denise
Levertov's poem 'Roast Potatoes' in *This Great Unknowing* (Bloodaxe Books,
Newcastle, 2001). In the same posthumous collection, Levertov's poem
'Feet', treats of the Disney-fication of Hans Christian Anderson's 'The
Mermaid'. Here, I have taken liberties with current news of international
conflict, Mermaid folklore and Classical Mythology—the ballad is a
collage of mermaid myths and sources from varied cultures and periods.
From Classical Mythology, the sea nymphs known as *Nereids*, are often
confused with *Sirens*, part bird / part women, whose function was anti-
thetical to the benign guidance of the *Nereids*. The name *Siren* translates
as 'those who bind with a cord' or 'those who wither'. The 'Mermaid'
herself is a post-Classical invention.

Persephone

I don't think she ate from hunger, so much
as regret;
    how, six months into the dark,
—the air in her lungs, the blood in her veins
getting thin—
she fell in love
     though not with Death himself,
but some bright shade
that might have been his double:

the scent of autumn, say, or how the frost
arrives from somewhere else and cannot be
accounted for;
     the trail a serpent leaves
in grass;
    the sudden chill
that fills a house where something has been squandered:

water and blood; a child's first beaker of milk;
the sunlit drops that scatter from a bowl
of grime and rennet, where a silent flock
of neighbour women wash a bloodied corpse;
the inky line of vinegar and sweat
that trickles back along a soldier's wrist
and pools between the tunic and the skin.

The seeds were dark and sour,
and touched with bone;
she took them, not as food, but sacrament;
and later, when she hurried back to find
her mother's house, the land was beautiful,

not as it was, but as it should have been
before the cold arrived, the gift of snow
erasing what she thought would live forever:
the early cherry, with the later plum,
the blushing apricot, and woolly peach
black in the green, then gold,
where they sprouted and perished
over and over again, to remain unspoken.

Eurydice

Late in the season
she gathered the last of the thyme,

chervil and flat-leafed parsley, rue
and tarragon;

and when the morning cold
turned green to black,

she hid the bite-mark
in a coil of hops

and walked away, the silence at her back
conclusive, where her footprints petered out

in random strands
of glycerine and amber.

No one would find her now;
no one would come;

no one would rescue her skin
from the blue of forever;

though later,
in the poems he would sing,

the man she no longer remembered
would follow her ghost

to the crushed-plum and rainwater scent
of the outer fencing,

mending a white he had learned
from the first days of frost,

and bearing her name in his mouth,
like an egg or a pebble.

Mules at Ystradginlais

'The ferry across the Styx is a once-in-a-lifetime ride!'—
your shoulders hunched as we imagined Charon's.
We hurried down to meet you—where

shadows of willow trees danced sage moves
above the river's edge—absorbed in
the bursting seedpods of all we had to say.

The foal was lodged beneath the gorse
upon the other bank, the star on its forehead
shining through the water, clear as fruit in aspic;
a fly in amber; the coloured heart of a child's marble.

Above, the mother nosed the water—wild narcissus.
If we noticed, we said nothing. Ignored the dead
and boarded laughing. You cracked the wine.
We soon were in our cups, happily drifting nowhere.

Narcissus (Einzelgänger)

When snow came
he left them behind
and continued walking:

no more unspecified Thou,
no hanging echo,

only the present tense
and the verb to be

—the verb, as in
being awake,
or *being lost*,

dawn at the edge of a clearing,
citrus and grey,

a rumour in the leaves
of something

almost, but not altogether
animal, a constant in the bone

inherited
from no one else's fall
but his: the apple

smudging on his palm
like chalk, or ash,
and when he turned away

the voice he heard
was nothing like the wind

singling him out
to carry the blue of forgetting.

Part Three

Poems of the Father

Terns hang high above the inlet, riding
the winds. They tuck their wings and fall
beak-first into the shingled bay.

Prey secure, they flap across the flats
toward me, cutting through
the moment, freed from thought.

I run my fingers over the binocular case
and trace its lines as though they might reveal
a map of somewhere distant I must go

to 'put things back in place'—your phrase.
I whisper your name, fluted, like a prayer
and try to conjure something I can hold.

Some linger in their father's nests;
I am circling over the vague speck
of your camouflaged hide.

II

He banked on hope to keep the brood together;
was never there for all those *major moments.*
Take that summer's day when bees were humming
across the fallen walls that lay in huddles
at the elm-rotted edge of the orchard:
the girl on the swing was twirling her ribbons;
unbalanced, fell and broke a leg. She rubbed
her eyes, as if she were waking from Rip Van Winkle's
dream. Her brother stuck a stick into the nest
of bees above her, blind to her pain
and inside the house, hot towels and water
hung on a trivet, while a woman in calico
shuffled into the backroom with the sag
of age, to deliver the stillborn baby.

III

The loganberries cropped in five year cycles
in their protected patch beside the yew

and so I only picked them with you twice:
once, a boy, bewildered by your spiel

on death, decay and annual renewal
and then, again, toward last summer's end.

You savoured their sweetness; their loose clusters
trained on wires to curb their trailing habits

and, in the act we shared of harvesting,
knew something of the thing we call 'our selves'

persists in conserving the yield: pears and plums;
tomatoes cut down from their twisting vines;

sunflower heads picked over for their seeds;
the beehives drained of honey in the orchard

and loganberries, big fat loganberries
burgeoning on the bush. Your favourite.

They stained our fingertips as claret would;
as if, though thornless, they had drawn our blood,

each uvula of fruit sticky with unction—
waiting for the spread of fungi; leaf fall;

the swelling of humus and pumpkin globes;
your lips already whitened, the cold set in.

IV

Cows like boulders punctuate the tumps—
black and white studs in a green cushion.

Through the anticipation of a dog rose
near bursting in thousands of buds;

through nettle spears and fences flagged
with the bunting of cleaver and wool,

the muscles of a roe deer flex in the hedge's lea.
Just a twitch of the nose betrays him,

tasting the scented wind. A watched deer
never stirs, then—blink and miss it—

disappears, stealing the stillness. He bucks
along the hedgerow flashing his tail;

turns Devon to the Serengeti; reminds me
you also now have vanished in a film of air.

The Blue Hour
homage to Joseph Beuys

I SHAMAN

He falls from the near edge of heaven, sweet in his garment of
ozone and smouldering hair

and speaking in tongues: a shape neither angel nor man

they wrap in felt and rennet till his soul

recovers, like the makings of a dream,

questions and forebears, the reasons for navigation.

This street, or any other. Plum trees; lilies; children. Look again and see the shadow in the shadow of the cypress.

For hundreds of miles the streetlamps stutter and burn. Walk to the edge of the garden, holding the knife. Listen for blackbirds; look for the coming rain.

Notice the sap on the blade, how it sings like blood.

III EARTH

This was the promise they made and did not keep. The faded diagrams; the terse instructions. Forebears and questions, suspended in radio static.

Where do the butterflies go, when the day is ended?

Where is the soul while its vessel waits to be healed?

IV PSYCHE

They wanted to become the other world, shrouding their bodies in woolskins and burning feathers.

They wanted to touch the wind, to soar like the hawk.

They would have made the journey, then chosen to return, the salt of the ether bright on their lip and hands, the angel of distance swaddled in felt and dripping.

V TERREMOTO

Home again, he waits to be revealed. Tramcars and street trees; cafes and public gardens.

He feels the earthquake in a stranger's blood.

An angel uncurls from his hands, like a test tube, falling.

This is a dream I have from time to time. I fall asleep in the quiet of afternoon and wake in the blue hour, hazy and dusted with amber. The house is still; the world is a hairsbreadth away. I go to the window and, knowing before I look, I see that Lazarus is there, a shadow in the shadows of the cypress.

Later I wake—and this is the blue hour I dreamed. My body is strangely sweet; hazy and dusted with amber. The house is still; the world is a hairsbreadth away. I go to the window and, knowing before I look, I see a garden in the summer dusk: the empty lawn, the shadows in the cypress. Plum trees and lilies, vanishing into the dark.

The Promise of Home

I WESTMINSTER BRIDGE AS 'THE BRIDGE OF LIES'

We meet each other half way, catch the sky
blush pink, like lovers on the *Bridge of Lies*
who come to hear inviolable proposals.
I start to ask, but look into the sun
and drop the thread of what I mean to say.
Its shadow sinks beneath the Thames's pull;
emerges elsewhere on the esplanade
as out of breath as me. The asking's done.
As when Romantic Masters flattened out
the middle ground before their landscapes rose
to castles set on crenulated heights,
the moment slips away toward St. Paul's.
You lift yourself, to whisper, onto toes,
sing 'Yes' into my left ear's ringing bowl.

Note: The Bridge of Lies, in Sibiu, Romania, a place to which lovers go to
  make their marriage proposals, because it is said that no lies may be told
  upon the bridge.

II ANNUNCIATION

Set your memories down between these rocks,
fuse your palms, recall a psalm
and find the landscape as it truly is:
a complex, spiritual map.

Like two boats dreaming of land
after months adrift at sea, I will turn
to you, or you will turn to me,
as a weathervane turns

and in the smoke of incense that we burn
unearth the tragic tone
and violent shade of myth:

'If you wish to conceive simply eat
these tablets of pregnancy clay
crudely embossed with the image of Christ.'

III REMEMBRANCE DAY

My life began again when she was born
like the blessing of a river opening
on an inland sea—fresh water into standing.
You felt it too, in different ways:
think of that time, eighteen months later,
as we strolled between the headstones
damp-through in the sun's mizzled blush,
our daughter leading us on in her red
coat—a poppy in the rain—and you said
that the thought of one or both of us 'going'
frightened you more now she was alive;
how death seemed more present *because*
of her birth, like a line of perspective
that resolves itself beyond the painting's limits.

IV IN LOVE WE SENSE THE BRIEFNESS OF OUR LIVES

like a shoreline seen from sea—
the promise of home and then, unsure,
becoming ever distant—a ripple
that stems from a dropped stone.
And yet it seems the past is close behind
like the boy and girl who entertain
their parents' guests, reluctantly,
when all they've ever dreamed about is
changing themselves into animals or birds,
lured by the siren of the unseen horizon
and the stories people tell of paths beyond;
lured by the migration of butterflies
departing like leaves falling upwards,
out of the shadows and into the light,
searching everywhere for signs of grace.

V LONELY LIGHT

The rain comes down in driving rods for hours
besieging us inside our homes.
We sit alone and listen to the choral birds,

imagine going out. Out into the light
that strikes the church and stretches fingers
of shadow across the evening's back;

out into 'the lonely light', your mother's phrase,
this hour when all things stand alone,
utterly themselves—

those oaks that jag the sky
like black coral in a sea of milk;
those hulks of livestock

scutted with dung,
outlined in black,
like figures in Japanese paintings;

out beneath an ember of sun
that is sliding now, ever quicker,
down the brow of a western hill.

VI TAKING IN THE TOMATO CANES FOR AUTUMN

The August sun pulsated like a heart
behind a gauze of rain as I continued
digging, cutting, slowly taking down
the framework of the season's growth:

the trellis of sweet peas; the lilies gone over—
and you, wisely, spending hours indoors
keeping the children busy with painting,
model making; calm as an inland sea—

that was when I knew, again, I believe
in you, and always so, the way we believe
in daybreak, the fall of night, turning tides;
the slow decline of rock-face into sand—

as I folded up the tomato canes
and stacked them in the garage for the autumn.

VII SAMHAIN

All leaf-fall week we let the pumpkin rest
on the courtyard's mossy steps. You carved
a Janus out of him—one face a cry,
the other smiling. Naked in its pot
the pinnate maple stretched its arms
to shelter him from tumbling red gum leaves.
Quinces, rosehips, autumn's roses; the slug
infested shells of rotting passion fruit—
these were all that clung on from the summer,
as I cling on to feeling this is how
I'll always come back home to you, shaping
pumpkins with the children and, when they've grown,
some other kind of love and, when they fly,
that grace turned face to face, to its own source.

VIII THE LANGUAGE NEST

You reason with our children in your mother's tongue—
gentle; laughter flying like flags—whilst mine
hefts its weight as if in a wood chopping logs.
When I am done with working it,
I sit on the steps of the temple
of your conversation and let it float
until your words are clouds and, theirs?
their words are cloud shadows
falling across the fells of my nature;
their answers more than grace notes
in this counterpoint of curiosity.
You have made of them bright insects,
buzzing, as if the swarm of words
gave warmth; a green light to the back of silence.

Homage to Henri Bergson

I RECURSIVE

It was the smell of paraffin
at night, during a storm,

made me imagine myself
this far in the future

remembering a child
I never was,

sitting up late
in a whisper of gas-pipes and snowfalls,

the flame in his mirror
blue as the promise of love.

II ÉLAN VITAL

It flowered earlier this year,
the meadowsweet,
lining the ditches along the Kinaldy road
with the dark and implacable perfume
of mourning;
                        not

the mourning that comes of a death,
or a needless loss,
but how the earth cries out to us
the stark reminder of a life to come,

just as this living flame of lace and dust
draws from the black of leaf-mould
and molten bone
its memory of how the light arrived,

not somewhere in the sky, not in the stars,
but far out in the streaming fields of grass
where something—bird, not bird—
began to sing.

III CHANCE

It takes us years to recognise the flaw:
poisons of various kinds and the cream-flavoured chill

of the christening gown;
flies at my father's hand, flies in his coat;

the cold boat on the machair
packed with song.

The year draws in: we rinse and shelve the dead;
the lower pasture flocks with wading birds;

and how will we live with cold, if not
apprenticed to the discipline of less,

accustomed to a luck we cannot say
is good or bad, but mostly nondescript:

the least mistake; the unexpected cry;
the scent the dead leave on a laundered sheet

after a morning's frost
or a wifeless summer.

IV ÉLAN VITAL

What can we do without? What wastes away?
milk tooth and apple, birthmark and powdered skin?
This morning, half-awake, I heard the foxes
calling to one another in the mist;
tonight, on the headland, a kill: that vapid wash
of shoulder-bone and fur, its unstitched smile
the last thing to decay in new-leafed grass; the first
to be re-entered in the holy book
of codes and psalms, become identical
with appleseed and skin, milk-teeth and water.

V TIME AND FREE WILL

I was thinking of somewhere else,
the country, say, of how things look for others:
towns glimpsed in transit; a playpark, those salt-coloured houses
where people like us are living a life like ours.

Yet how would that differ from absence, or being lost?
How would it differ from having you find me dead
some warm afternoon in the future, my eyes unstitched,
the one thing I left unfinished hanging for weeks
in the folds of the curtains, the bookshelves, the cold TV?

Think of those tiny hamlets, far in the woods,
those upland villages we never see
from passing trains or ferries to the mainland.
Think of a walnut tree in an empty meadow,
or cheese laid out in rows for the weekend market,

then think of ourselves going out, in a different weather,
the strangers we might have been and yet to each other
tender and fretted with touch in the cool of the morning,
and haunted by nothing, not even the thought of a haunting.

The Other Brother

There are dawns when he is up before me,
breathing quietly across the saltmarsh,
each foot placed carefully
                          from log to log
trying not to scare the waders —
                                  ibis,
egrets,
            blue herons on slow motion stilts —
who watch for fish
                      and dark figures like his:

a stone
            dislodged
                          and he knows the cranes —
motionless for now amongst the canes —

will rise
            in exuberant outbursts
                                      from the edge,
out across the bay where wave peaks gather
leading from nowhere to nowhere;

or is it more that, simply,
        I imagine him
                      some mornings
doing richer things than I;

on beaches where spoonbills nest;
purposeful along the long
north-reaching thumb
                        of the Ness,
straight as a sheldrake's flight;

buoyed by the morning's shiftings;

the island of the day as yet
        uninhabited;
                    the wharves
draped in the promise of work;

reaching his eyes
                    into open sky,

or over silted waters in the marsh,
grasping for a hold amongst these things:

the flight of cranes—
        their slow and even turning—
                    released to light at the water's edge,

across the groynes
        that serrate the skyline;
across the seam that breaks
                    the sky from sea,
the sea with its mixture of welcomes
        and warnings?

II MY DESERT BROTHER

His land, like his language, is crazed:
>> its whip-like *ocotillos* and thorny *mesquites*
>>> startling in their profusion, casting islands of shade

over desert *mariposas*; *palominos* veering
>> into *paloverde* trees
>>> kicking ideas aside; disturbing the secrets of air.

His road has tightened to a band of black;
>> its cinders cascading in every direction—
>>> tail guard of a speeding car.

Sometimes it fails him—this world
>> and the words to which it is tethered—
>>> though often it is he who fails to notice

that things alone, not words, have led to what
>> he knows. They come out of nowhere—
>>> things in their homes—

as lightly as shadows: an unnamed animal
>> dying on the sun-baked earth;
>>> hoof over rock; dust on their heels;

his own shape vanishing
>> into unknown territories.
>>> Ring of a shovel on rocks.

III MY BROTHER AUDUBON

The bird he sees and the bird he draws
are one. Which begs an inner silence,
shifting from the world of words
to the language of tone and line.

He must forget the names he knows—
neither 'tail' nor 'wing', nor 'beak' nor 'claw'—
and simply move along the edge of each,
with his eye set in his pencil-tip,

thinking of no sound at all—save that of ink
on paper—to catch the truth
of their existence, out there, in the world.

A buzzard flaps overhead,
clutching something dead.
He catches it in chiaroscuro.

IV HERON CHICK

We stepped into morning
through snaggles of moss
        and toadstools,

our memories of the times
        we'd been before

laid out beneath us
        like flagstones in a path.

Evidence of otters—
a pair we knew
were somewhere round—

in the form of fish heads,
abandoned on the verge.

You pushed through
thickets of Indian Balsam
clogging the bank,
their swollen seedpods
                        going off
like strings of firecrackers—

a kingfisher clattered by in blue,
hunting dace and minnow—

and I stood back,
looking through
        the swathe you'd cut
                in them.

There was the heron chick,
bedded down between the rotting logs—

broken, its wing
          and its legs . . .

'Nature is a common link,' they say,
so why would *You* or *I* lift up a hand

to put the chick out of its misery,
while the other argued we should simply leave

with no interference at all? In spite
of all the things we both might choose to say,

both ways were the same;
          and *there* lay our bond.

V SCATTERING MY BROTHER'S ASHES

The sea pulled us through an interior
of tractors turning perfect furrows open
to seagulls flocking in their hundreds, worming;

down to a bay where we walked untouched
sand, alone, save for the tracks of waders
and distant children dipping nets for schools
of fingerlings in the shadows of rocks.

Hopeful boats hung on the mud bars, waiting
for the tide to rise and take them out
into the crescent of the sky-mirroring sea.

The sun lay low—falling in erratic islands
of light. You tipped and emptied the urn
with a fierce grief—a moment of oneness—
knowing that by evening the estuary would turn.

Towards a Book of Common Prayer

'Our poetry now is the realization that we possess
nothing. Anything therefore is a delight . . .'
                            —JOHN CAGE

I

Begin with a word for blue

—the progress of a shadow on a lawn, or silver tracking on an
outhouse door where snails have gathered in a well of shade—

nothing replaces the colours of childhood:
citrus and inkstains, the leaf between butter and amber,
all the subtleties we cannot name for sure,

snowfall on water; earth tints; degrees of shading.
The green in the woods like the green in the blue of your eyes.

II

Daybreak   or snow   brings them out:

cloistered   and strange to the light

they cross a graveyard   or a harrowed field

one at a time
            or together
                        in hurried pairs

nothing unusual in that
                        as they come to resemble

curlew or rabbit   weasel or rust-coloured deer

yet now and then
                through drifts of mist or ice

we see them in the shapes we cannot name

and nothing we can do will bring them home

no sympathetic charm   no wistful kill

III

The way a song-thrush hammers at the window with neither
    fear nor urgency,
its bewilderment momentary and soft, betrayed by the smaller
    light we set against a darkness that has yet to fall;
almost, but not altogether losing its place in the glow of
    happenstance,
which is all it can ever know, and is all there is.

IV

Suddenly I remember the name for this wave of goldfinches
tracking the verge of a country road at the summer's end;

and this is the one clue I have to the fact that I am waiting for
something else to happen:
nothing I could fear, or hope for: *something else*;
not much to go on, though what I need now is less.

I stop at the brow of a hill where the late sun whitens and swells;
I listen for a shadow in the woods;
not much to go on, but this is the art of waiting:

making my pact with nowhere and sounding it out;
the moment when darkness begins to fall and I hear the singing;
the chill in the grass; the dewfall; the startled dark.

V

(the holy land)

Yes, I remember the maps and how they were wrong:

the land they forgot; the children; the unpruned vines;
the dream between one household and the next;

bonfires; alleys; catwalks; laundry rooms;

the unofficial pharmacies and schools;
the drift and flow of women's conversations;
the drift and flow of chants and skipping rhymes;

the long continuum of touch and fire
that history replaces with itself:

a jug of water; moonlight in a room;
an empty bed where someone should be sleeping.

VI

(Gujari: Absence)

No damage; only the mysteries of separation.
Fruit in a bowl; clouds on a yellowing field.

Fragments of blue and grey and the promise of amber.
What happens in absence, when nothing should happen but
time.

A gull at the edge of vision, apart from the flock,
lifting its head as if it would answer a question.

To wait for an end is to wait for another beginning.

Echoes of last year's rain and the ochre of distance.
The thought of a downfall reserved for another season.

~

Not fonder   so much as larger

                              heart and world

expanding   as a parish under snow
or autumn flood

                                   expands:

the distances immense from thought to thought
from field to field   from tree to greening tree;

until (at last) we choose to speak
of roses   or the silence after rain
that opens to reveal   another house:

what (yesterday)   was really little more
than cups and chairs

                       a book

                              a bowl of light
is something other now

                       the limitless

                              the lost.

VII

Though surely these were forbidden:
whispers of colour
buried in paint pots and crayon,
ochre and crimson lake, leaf-green and umber.

I ghosted my name in pencil
on test-sheets and jotters,
ghosted commandments and laws
and quadratic equations,

the letters fading as I turned the page
and every blank a promise till I made
my mark:
                a promise, innocent as snow,

or like the moment when I raised the lid
and foundered on the calm of Prussian blue,
the sudden latitude of Chinese white
where nothing seemed more possibility

than absence,
like that echo in the hall
where voices disappeared
through repetition,

catcalls and nicknames
vanishing into the distance,
leaving me empty and true
at the foot of the stairs.

VIII

We hadn't prepared for this

                        the glimmer of wings

and the shore road blurring with sand

in an April wind;

just we're never prepared

for the soul when it comes

an owl face stitched to the dark

                        a sudden light

or how a stairwell fills

                some cloudless night

with something like a held breath

                        or a voice

about to speak

                the wishes we never surrendered

the flesh we concealed

come true at last

                like prophecies

                        or dreams

IX

(media vita)

One of those nights: late summer; the Japanese anemones
      pale in the dark,
but visible, blush-pink and white when I sit up late,
unable to sleep, alone in my tidy kitchen;

and all at once I see it has already started:
that afterwards I couldn't quite imagine back in high school,
when the point of being here was being *young*;

although, no longer young, I'm not quite as old as I'd thought

and not at all resigned, or wise,
as I vowed to be
if I should come to this: a stick-thin soul
grown innocent, a near-
impeccable and undemanding creature of the shadows

pressed to a rainy window   watching the stars
and tuned entirely to another wavelength

where nothing happens but the shift of tides
and something empty, turning in the wind,
beyond desire
        beyond what might have been.

X

(Arivaca)

We know how the dead are replaced:
moths at the porch light; bobcats scouting the wash;
a cluster of Inca doves in the yellow of dawn;

but nothing fills the gap left by the living:
they linger in a mist of creosote
or vanish once more on a back road sweetened with rain.

We know how the dead are dismissed
and how they return

like migrant birds with sea routes in their bones,
angles of wind and nothingness locked in the spine,

but, tender as the flesh where thorns begin,
pale as the wind in the bones of a dead saguaro,

the living disappear and leave no sign.

∽

                    The living disappear
and leave no sign:

scarcely recalling the souls they expected to be,
whiling themselves away through the gold afternoons

or, haunted by a shadow in the mirror,
they gather, like a feather from the air,
the promise of someone else—soul friend and stranger—

a creature formed of emptiness and light
turning to see itself, beyond recognition,

casual and mildly surprised, as if it has come
by accident, and means to slip away

a red-tailed hawk, a hooded oriole,

vanishing back to the sky
before anyone sees.

XI

(coed)

I drive north through squalls of rain sunlight between the
    clouds and a sudden
blindness   as the windscreen blurs and whitens

the headlamps in the mirror far and bronzed: half-
circus   half a memory of light
from childhood   all those hill-farms glimpsed through rain
that looked so much   like home
(the private gold   the blur of permanence)

though sometimes we found our way to something else
making whatever we could
of coal tar   wireless   instruments of bone.

I think of that coastal woodland when I sleep:
the green in the black of the world   the black in the green

how   sooner or later   it settles for birdsong and thaw

and how the evening smells   as I cross the sands

a child again   no more the self I was
than starlight   or the ghost in iodine.

XII

There is something to understand in an empty house

more than the unexpected weight
of solitude   the absence on the stairs
that ripens through the night hours   like a plum

or how the body tenses for a sound
it never hears   a slow fall in the blood

that might as well be ash   or drifting snow

some angle of forgetting   or the lack
that forms between the palate and the tongue.

No matter what it is we think we missed
we know ourselves as light

and how there is another in the room
when no one else is there   a hatchling shape

imagined all along   the body's chill
and unrequited echo in a world

where everything is purest accident:
          its parallels and opposites implied

in shadows   slut's hair
          thumbprints etched in glass

On the Road to the Eye Hospital

On a warm afternoon,
when an old wind blows through your face,
old as the grass in the meadows, old as the stones,
older than any memory you harbour,

think of the stories they tell
when vision is lost,
how everything there is begins as song:
water and earth and fire, and the kingdom of air

imagined from the sound a blind man hears
when the wind picks him out
like the heartbeat he finds in a mirror,

picks him out tendon by tendon, and thought by thought,
a fabric of echoes, unwound from the moment of grace,
and shaped to the curve of itself by the curve it is not.

Dedications

'Some Notes on a Theory of Emergence' is for Dennis O'Driscoll

'In Conversation' is for Anthony Wilson

'A Horse's Skull' is for Robin Robertson

'*Los ángeles mohosos*' is for Luis Muñoz

'The Ice Pool Under the Church Tower' is for David Morley

'Prayer / Why I am Happy . . .' is for Laurie Brown

'Diving on the Atoll' is for Gavin Shelton

'Mules at Ystradginlais' is for Paul Clark

'The Blue Hour' is for Diana Weilepp

'The Other Brother' is for Susan Mills and Alison Barnett

'The Promise of Home' is for May Snothel

'Westminster Bridge as the *Bridge of Lies*' is dedicated i.m. Robert Woof